Leadership

Work On Your Ability To Communicate, Steer Out Of
Uncomfortable Situations, And Have Indirect Influence
Over Others

*(A Guide For Businesses On Placing An Emphasis On Long-
term Development Over Short Term Gains)*

JochenHaberl

TABLE OF CONENT

What Is It That We Have To Make?

One essential question that has not been addressed up to this point is, "What do you make?" How do you ascertain what it is that the customer wants and then fulfil that requirement? Because you are tasked with locating the solutions to these problems, you are in the position that you are now in. Everyone here is working hard to locate the things that customers are most interested in purchasing.

WHAT DOES IT APPEAL TO THE CONSUMER TO HAVE?

That is the question that needs to be answered. It is difficult to find an answer, and even if found, that answer rarely remains the same. It adapts and undergoes metamorphosis. The list of positive attributes could go on and on: organic, low fat, good gas mileage, etc.

The fact that the customer might not know the answer either adds an interesting twist to the situation.

How do you come to that conclusion?

You have two primary directions that you can go in:

Analyse the feedback received on the product thus far.

Make an effort to innovate new products.

The strategies that you employ for the two different categories are likely to be significantly different from one another.

EXISTING PRODUCT COMMENTS AND SUGGESTIONS

A product that is presently available on the market is evaluated to determine whether or not it is possible to make it "better." Better can mean a multitude of things, including the following:

Enhancement of the product's quality in an effort to eliminate customer complaints.

Less spending means a higher profit margin.

Altering the size in order to attract more clients.

Adjustments were made to the formulation in order to boost performance.

Extending the shelf life of a product in order to cut down on the amount of money lost due to it going bad.

These are just a few instances of the numerous ways in which a product might be altered in response to comments made by customers.

If you already have a well-known brand or product on the market, this can be very risky water to tread in (go back to the example of CokeR from earlier), and you run the risk of driving away your existing consumer base. This sense of estrangement can become even more pronounced if the product's packaging includes a number of supplementary certifications or messages that provide value additions.

Products made from organic ingredients are one example of this. If you develop a product that is 100% organic and then decide to take the certification off of the product because it costs too much to make given the ingredients, you are in for a bumpy road.

People purchase organic goods for a variety of reasons, one of which is the belief that they are of superior quality and provide a higher level of protection against foodborne illness. It is not my purpose to determine whether or not what you say is accurate; it is not the focus of this conversation. For the aforementioned reasons, customers buy the aforementioned products. When they learn that you have altered a certification, you run the risk of losing them permanently.

Before making significant alterations to a product or even a service, the vast majority of businesses first conduct extensive market research. They are going to employ a firm or bring in a group of consumers to act as focus group participants in order to collect input. Several iterations of the modification are discussed, and the responses to these discussions are evaluated to determine whether or not the change constitutes an improvement.

If the modification is substantial enough, corporations may test it in a small market in the field to see how it compares to the conventional product in order to determine whether or not to implement it more broadly. These kinds of methodical approaches can be of great use in modifying or enhancing a product in a variety of ways. In circumstances like this, exercising extreme caution is a prudent strategy.

Setting The Scene

The development of a growth mindset, which is critical to the success of both you and your team in the long run, is made possible primarily through coaching.

Preparation is necessary for every single coaching session! Maintain an open mind and listen with full attention. Keep in mind that you should be listening four times for every time you talk. When you go beyond that, you are no longer coaching; you are teaching. The best coaches are aware of their own prejudices and understand how each player fits into the larger picture. A good coach will help others grow while directing them towards the purposes and goals of the firm.

Whenever you are coaching, make sure to be present in the moment and have the acronym STOP in mind:

Talking very slowly

Voice inflection: a lower level than is typical for speaking.

Questions and a stance that are open

Make sure to maintain eye contact and active listening during this pause.

Instilling confidence and leading to good changes in performance are both outcomes that can be achieved by cultivating a thriving atmosphere. In order to be a good coach, you need to have a relationship with the person you are guiding. Warning to avoid the temptation to remedy the situation. It is important to keep in mind that a member of your team is not damaged.

How do you determine when it is appropriate to coach? Coaching is aimed to bring about changes in behaviour. Consider these elements to be modifiable risk factors or things that are within our control to alter. A person's weight, food, level of physical activity, reaction to a given circumstance, and so on are all examples of aspects of themselves that are within their control to alter.

Utilising the GROW model as a coaching tool is a speedy approach. In the 1980s, Sir John Whitmore and Graham Alexander devised the GROW model, which later went on to have a number of different iterations.

In order to get a better understanding of the ramifications, let's look at each part of the GROW method:

Goals

Determine the long-term as well as the short-term goals for coaching. The desired change in behaviour should be viewed as the long-term objective. The objectives for each individual coaching session make up the short-term goals. Keep in mind that there will be more than one session required for this coaching procedure.

Consider the end goal of the coaching session before beginning to work with a certain individual. What do you consider to be the positive results? Which behaviour would you like to see changed the most?

Take into consideration your management goals in relation to the behaviour that you want to change. Is it a trait that can be changed, or is it something that comes naturally to that person? Characteristics of a person's personality cannot be changed. However, these components present the chance for the individual to have a better awareness of how the characteristics they possess are seen by others.

Have you, for instance, ever come across a person who asserts, "I know I am/can be___ (fill in the blank)"? Although this is something that comes naturally to the individual, they are aware that it may present difficulties for other people.

Now, think about goals that are reasonable for the coachee. Their observations should direct them towards a personal goal that contributes to the accomplishment of the manager's long-term objective.

When you develop goals for yourself, be sure they are SMART:

S is for "specific": what are your goals, exactly?

M is for measurable: how will you evaluate your level of success?

A is for attainable; what actions are you going to take?

Relevant question: are you able to explain your ideal world?

T = Time-bound: by what point do you anticipate having accomplished your objective?

Think about the objectives, ensure that they are SMART, and then write them down.

Who Do We Aspirationally Want To Be As A Group?

During the excruciatingly beautiful weeks of summer camp, the squad endured two practises a day in addition to playbook study and lunches in between. As a result, we all experienced significant amounts of sweating, bruising, and bleeding. We were welcomed each morning by the ever-present fragrance of cured tobacco that enveloped Winston-Salem. This aroma was spread across the city by the RJ Reynolds tobacco firm, which had a significant presence in the city. The odour, the heat, and the humidity were just some of the elements that were a part of the event, which also included arduous drill after arduous drill. Every night, we had a meeting with the coaches, and during those meetings, they discussed the previous day's performance and the obstacles that needed to be addressed the next day. The coaches had meticulously planned out each individual day in order to transform the collection of individuals into a cohesive unit that shared a same goal and was fully invested in the team's performance. At the end of each of these evening practises, our head coach would have a conversation with us.

His words, together with the manner in which he spoke them, were a wonderful source of motivation for me. Instead of letting the team's history or sports writers to define us, he chose to do it himself by delivering a few key messages that became ingrained in the group's personality and became a part of the team's identity. One of these messages was "NEVER, NEVER, NEVER GIVE UP," and it quickly became a mantra that would be used throughout the forthcoming season as a statement of encouragement to be repeated frequently. The Wake Forest football programme had historically finished last in the rankings and had won only one of the previous season's 12 games. In addition, the programme has never finished higher than last place. The preseason predictions for the 1979 season saw Wake finishing in last place in the conference once again.

Since the head coach was a graduate of Wake Forest himself and had played for the Demon Deacons in the past, he focused on creating in us a sense of pride in our school and a spirit of reliance upon each other as a member of the team. The squad had been putting in arduous work all summer, and they were finally ready to call it a night after reaching their mental and physical breaking point. On that particular day, conflicts had broken out between members of the team as they were practising, and the coaches were yelling and screaming at each other.

It was clear that Coach had recognised the significance of this day in determining the makeup of our team for the upcoming season. He went over all of the positive qualities and the talent on this year's squad. These were talents and character traits that we probably couldn't see in ourselves, and we certainly weren't looking to see them in our state of weariness. He talked about all of the positive strengths and the talent on this year's team. He spoke about how proud he was of us because of how hard everyone had worked throughout the off-season and how prepared everyone was when they arrived at summer camp. He said this because of how hard everyone had worked during the off-season. He told us that we had to make a decision about who this team would be for this season right then and there, in that room, and not just as individuals but as a cohesive whole. He admitted that the day's tensions and disagreements had been a factor and said, "Today our energy, our enthusiasm, and our focus on making sure no one on this team fails took a huge dip." There is no one to blame for this situation who is not currently present in this room. To determine who is to blame for today's performance, all we need to do is take a quick glance in the mirror and then take a look around the room. Nobody outside of this room will have the ability to characterise who we are. No one else is going to decide whether we win or lose a game, carry out our responsibilities, or encourage us to be the best that we can be!

Maintain Your Self-Respect

Being professional is an essential component of effective leadership. There are several different approaches that you can take in order to give off an air of professionalism. Several instances are provided down below.

Dress Appropriately - Many establishments have dress standards that members are expected to abide with. Make sure that you follow these guidelines to the letter so that the other members of your team can see how vitally important it is to have appropriate attire. In addition to this, it bolsters your reputation and emphasises the fact that you take your professional responsibilities seriously.

Rather than trying to become friends with the individuals they supervise, some leaders focus instead on running productive meetings. Even while this may appear to be an excellent plan, it's possible that it's not the most effective technique to manage a group of people. It is possible for meetings to devolve into social gatherings during which little actual work is accomplished. Because the leader is spending too much time trying to win everyone else's approval, significant topics are not brought up for discussion.

To prevent this from happening, develop an agenda that will assist you in maintaining your organisation throughout the duration of the meeting. Be sure to maintain command of the talks while also allowing others the opportunity to contribute their thoughts. Directing the conversation back to what needs to be discussed in a planned manner should be done whenever it strays from the topic at hand. You may say something along the lines of, "That is a very intriguing story. Now, back when we were talking about..." If you do this, you can make sure that the meeting accomplishes what it set out to do without giving the members of your team the impression that they were reprimanded in any way.

Sessions of Effective Coaching Should Be Conducted Successful coaching sessions help you address the behaviours of your team. You have the chance to reinforce positive performance and redirect any obstacles that arise as a result of this opportunity. But in order to accomplish this, you must first ensure that you have all of the necessary items.

Bring any reports that you might need to refer to during the session with you. This will prevent you from having to leave or pause the coaching session in the middle to get data. You should also make sure that you select an area where you and the other member of your team can discuss without being interrupted or distracted by anything else.

You want your team to have the feeling that they are crucial to the team's success, and having effective coaching sessions may drive this point home.

Enhance Your Capabilities in Communication

To be an effective leader, you need to have excellent communication abilities. This is a prerequisite for becoming a leader. This encompasses anything from being able to articulately express objectives to actively listening to what other people on your team have to offer. When it comes to becoming a leader, having strong communication skills will go you a long way. The following are some suggestions that will assist you in enhancing the level of communication that you have with your team:

The Bible Offers Leadership Lessons.

You have, most likely on multiple occasions, read the Bible. You have probably listened to a number of sermons and messages that have focused on various books and passages from the Bible. You are aware that maintaining a connection with the Lord on a spiritual level is beneficial for you. When you are in need of solace or when you are praying, you might reflect on it.

However, is there anything in the Bible that may teach us about leadership?

The answer is unequivocally and unequivocally yes.

Many people have made the effort to find an answer to this question, and many of them have discovered various notions of leadership and management from the Bible. The Bible has the potential to and actually does teach us about Leadership. When we consider that "influence is all that leadership is, nothing more and nothing less," this becomes an even more important point.1

Learning leadership skills from the Bible can be done in a number of different ways. The author of this book takes a "Not-So-With-You" stance. Why was it necessary for Jesus to deliver such a specific instruction? That line of reasoning is what propels the first section of the book forward. We look at how power is used and abused in the Bible to sketch out God's leadership; we look at what values the Bible has taught us and our leaders to imbibe and live; we look at how the follower, not the leader, should be the primary focus of leadership; and we look at a concept called success versus significance.

Come on, and get ready to dig in.

11 DO NOT STOP GROWING YOUR SKILL SET IN ANY WAY

True managers never stop learning new things, and they never give up when faced with a new issue; instead, they embrace it with excitement.

They are eager to increase both the breadth and depth of their knowledge and expertise at all times.

They have trouble sitting idle and spend all of their free time reading, training, attending refresher courses, and researching ways in which they can increase both their own productivity and that of their staff.

They have the insight to see beyond, anticipating conditions that could hinder the firm's future performance, while constantly continuing to appreciate and invest in their strengths. This is true even when the company is performing well.

Because the world is in a state of perpetual change and because continuously reinventing oneself is necessary in order to stay up with the competition, it is no longer possible to preserve the status quo by being stationary.

Never rely key decisions on the organisational structure of the company; rather, modify this structure in order to suit the requirements imposed by the market.

In order for this to be possible, the structure must be malleable and able to adjust itself to meet the various requirements that may crop up at any given point in time.

At any point in your life, you should make an effort to locate a guide or an example to emulate who is capable of imparting knowledge to you. Every one of us owes a debt of gratitude to the various people who have helped shape our lives along the road, beginning with our parents and grandparents and continuing on to our professors, coworkers, and, of course, our managers. We never stop learning, and there is always someone who can teach us something, regardless of our age: having a role model to strive to is essential in order to enable us to continually get better.

Never allow yourself to believe that you have reached your goals.

Even if you have worked your way to the top of the organisation, you will still need someone to show you the way, even though you are the one who should be setting the example for your colleagues.

Always ask yourself, "Who is my mentor right now?" and if you can't come up with an answer, you should take cover as quickly as possible.

Everyone needs someone they can look up to and model their behaviour after, or at the very least get inspiration from, in order to continuously grow and develop.

The training that you receive as a team leader is equally as vital as the training that your employees receive.

Companies can only expand in the event that the individuals who work there do so as well. If you don't invest in your employees' training, the vast majority of them will cease using their brains and will become entirely unmotivated.

A firm that makes the decision to reduce or, even worse, eliminate its budget for employee training is a corporation that is doomed to fail in the future. Once they become aware of it, it will be too late for them to do anything about it.

You shouldn't be scared to surround yourself with good and capable people for the simple fear that they might one day take your place in the company; but, you should make sure that their success will secure your own personal and professional progress within the organisation.

Where Are the Limits? Do I have a dog with me?

If I were to release him from his confinement, I have no idea what mischief he may get into. I would be responsible for any damage caused by his teeth. If he were to bite someone, I would be the one liable for the medical care of the victim. And if he were to get out, he might travel a great distance, and I wouldn't have any idea where he might end up.

Therefore, I confine him with a fence.

What are the repercussions of my actions in this regard?

To begin, I don't have to be concerned about him anymore. He is currently in his cage. He has things in there to protect him and keep him engaged at the same time. He has access to both food and water. And whenever he has something that needs my attention, he will bark at me to get it.

People are not animals, that much is obvious. However, this serves as a valuable lesson. There is a certain amount of freedom that comes with being aware of what you can and cannot do. You don't waste your time worrying so much about options that aren't really possible, do you? Isn't it true that being prepared for whatever that life throws at you and having a plan for how to handle it gives you peace of mind?

A Few Words Regarding the Enforcement

Obviously, the effectiveness of rules is directly proportional to how strictly they are enforced. This is the point at which leaders are sometimes required to make difficult decisions. When the regulations that are supposed to be followed in black and white are broken, there should be clear repercussions. If for no other purpose, but to instill dread in those who would intentionally violate the policy, the sanctions for policy violations should be less apparent.

In addition, rules offer a framework within which the quality of someone's work can be evaluated. If she performs exceptionally well, and you quantify this, you have an excellent opportunity to call attention to it, don't you think?

You will also have the option to fix areas that are in need of improvement thanks to the regulations. If you're on top of things, hopefully you'll be able to offer support to someone who needs it before the situation escalates into a serious issue.

And finally, rules serve as a solid foundation upon which to educate newly hired employees.

The Various Ways In Which Rules Can Assist You In Getting The Most Out Of Your Organisation

As we've seen, following rules can help your organisation in three different ways.

To begin, they have the potential to enhance people's ability to perform their tasks. When you have a clear understanding of what you can and cannot accomplish, it is much simpler to get things done.

Second, having rules eliminates the need for arguments to take place over matters that are already resolved. This will enable more time to be spent on things that are more productive.

Thirdly, they give managers a structure that they may use to improve how they do their own job of evaluating the performance of their employees.

Create a formal set of guidelines right now if you don't already have one.

If you do, you should check their accuracy at regular intervals to ensure that they are up to current.

If you do that, you'll unleash the potential of your employees to turn your vision into a reality.

Chapter 4: Strive to Fulfil the Needs of All Stakeholders

The majority of leadership occupations still require interaction with superiors or other individuals in higher-ranking positions. Because they are responsible for monitoring the work of the leaders, we can also refer to bosses as overseers.

For the vast majority of business managers, for instance, the CEO or one of the other executives of the company serves in the capacity of overseers. The majority of people who are self-employed have clients who act as their supervisors. Even the CEO of a firm is required to interact with the company's shareholders and make certain that the shareholders are satisfied with the company's revenues.

The majority of leadership responsibilities include striking a balance between the desires and requirements of those who exercise oversight and those of those who are led. At the end of the day, the only thing that the typical worker is concerned about is his or her wage, for example. They can be concerned about the time they get off work or the amount of days they have off from work as well.

On the other hand, in a typical company, the typical overseers, which include executives and shareholders, want to see an increase in earnings. They aim to get the most out of each person in terms of both time and production, and they want to achieve this as much as possible. The primary obstacle that stands in the way of an organization's progress towards success is, the vast majority of the time, a conflict in the interests of the overseers and the followers.

Reduce the overseers' expectations as much as possible.

As soon as you are in a position of leadership, you should make every effort to assume command of the requirements imposed by your superiors. If you are meeting with shareholders to discuss profit estimates, for instance, you should warn them that the upcoming year is going to be challenging for the company financially. If you need to organise an event for the organisation, when you meet with the people in charge of supervising the event, be sure to emphasise how tough it will be to organise the event.

Over prepare for the task that is currently before you.

However, this does not imply that you should decrease your standards or perform below your potential. Even if you have been successful in lowering the expectations of the supervisor, you must continue to put in a lot of effort. You are still need to demonstrate to them a strategy outlining how you intend to attain the objective that has been set by the organisation. You should not, however, give the overseers permission to set goals and objectives that are difficult to achieve. Your followers will have a difficult time achieving ambitions and goals of this nature. If the goals are too challenging, you may need to subject your followers to a life of servitude at their place of employment in order to achieve them. Because of this, people won't like you as much. It is to everyone's advantage to hold higher-ups to a lesser standard.

Deliver results that are superior to those anticipated by the supervisors.

If you were able to lessen the expectations of the overseers, the next stage is to over-deliver on the promise that you made. If you do so, you will increase your chances of receiving bonuses for your productivity as well as awards for meeting quotas. You will be successful in meeting the supervisors' expectations since they have been scaled down to a level that is more reasonable. You also increase your popularity among your followers as a result of their success due of how you have guided them.

If the expectations are too great, you should avoid taking on leadership duties.

A boss who assumes control of a company while the economy is thriving is guaranteed to fail in their role. The numbers of items sold typically increase when the economy is doing well. As a result of increased profits, supervisors' quotas and expectations also increased significantly. At this point, it is quite unlikely that new leaders will be able to successfully lessen the expectations of the overseers.

During these challenging times, it will be more difficult for new leaders to assume leadership positions. When the "bust" phase of the boom-bust cycle begins, you will be blamed for the failure of the company to accomplish its goals, despite the fact that the organisation never had the opportunity to reach its goals to begin with. This is because the boom part of the cycle occurred before the bust part. You are going to be made the scapegoat by the firm and the overseers so that they may save face in front of the general public and in front of their employees.

You run the risk of irreparably damaging your reputation, and people will view you as a loser as a result of your mistake. They will not take into account the fact that the odds were stacked against you when you took on the job of leader. They will just concentrate on the fact that you failed.

Instead, you ought to time your entry into the leadership roles during a period of the organization's downtime so as to maximise your chances of success. It is much simpler for a talented coach to create his or her reputation when working with a lower-ranked team, for instance, when taking a job in the coaching profession. If he is given command of a team that is in the running for the championship, then any result that falls short of winning the title will be regarded as a failure. If the coach decides to keep a losing squad, a successful season will be defined as any finish that is higher than the team's rating from the prior year.

If you are just starting out in a leadership role, this method of approach to leadership is the one that will serve you best. It is preferable to lead and enhance organisations that are not operating well to achieve glory.

Is Leadership A Trait That Can Be Passed Down?

It has been said quite a few times that leadership is sometimes a quality that is passed down from one generation to the next. To illustrate this point further, let's look at an example:

Illustration A: Imagine that you are the son of a man who was once the most accomplished expert in his area. As a leader, your father was engaged in various positive activities. Therefore, there are a lot of expectations placed on you as well, most notably from the people who are a part of the community or the group in which your father used to hold the position of leader.

An important question is about to be asked: are you certain that you will be able to lead as effectively as your father did in the past, or not? Are you going to let the enormous expectations hold you back, or are you going to be ready to take the leadership to the next level?

Scientists believe that because you received your father's genes, you have the potential to be an effective leader. You should have the same qualities that your father did, but there are many people who will say that there are a lot of leaders whose sons couldn't prove themselves as leaders in any aspect of their lives. Despite this, you are expected to have those qualities. If that is the case, then the son of every renowned leader would have either been a great leader or a good leader, and this would have resulted in the creation of a large number of famous leaders. If the same idea is correct, then every king's son would have gone on to rule his own country, and all of the kingdoms would have maintained their previous levels of power and prosperity. When we examine this idea from the perspective of how things actually work, we find that it cannot possibly be right.

It is not required for an ordinary man who aspires to hold a position of authority to have the traits of leadership that were passed down to him by his parents. To become a fantastic leader, all he needs to do is be a man who possesses a number of admirable traits. Therefore, leadership is not solely a characteristic that is passed down from generation to generation; on the contrary, it is a quality that can be found in anyone. The qualities of risk taking, courageousness, articulation, and motivation are all traits that may be seen in him by him, any of his teachers, his parents, or any of the people that love him like his parents. If someone possesses these qualities, which are the criteria of a leader, then that person has the potential to be an excellent leader.

Again, certain real-life experiences reveal that there are many people who possess the same virtues that their fathers did, and these attributes were passed down from generation to generation. For instance, there are a lot of people whose dads were brilliant writers, and a lot of those people's children have followed in their footsteps. Given that he and his father share many of the same characteristics, it is reasonable to assert that the two of them are comparable. They are the only ones who can carry on the legacy left by their parents in their own right. One question that has not been satisfactorily resolved is whether or not leadership ability is a trait that can be passed down from one generation to the next. Both of these interpretations are valid for understanding it. Therefore, a more in-depth explanation is still required for the purpose of providing an answer to this question.

5 The Dynamics of the Team

The dynamics of a team or group are an extremely essential duty, and it is the leader's job to be responsible for how the members of the group engage with each other and communicate with one another. Larger issues can arise as a result of a failure on the part of the leader to develop or support favourable group dynamics. This is the point at which cracks can begin to emerge inside your team. You, as the leader, need to pay attention to the manner in which your team communicates not just with you, but also with one another and with the other members of the team.

To accomplish this, you must first become familiar with the capabilities and limitations of each member of the team. Only then can you determine who on the team will complement one another and who will not. There are times when the thought crosses our minds that if we only put our two top employees on the same team, they will produce excellent results. Working together, our third and fourth best employees won't necessarily produce the desired results for us. When you combine members one and four of the team with members two and three of the team, the total performance of the team improves. As leaders, we have a responsibility to take a comprehensive look at our results and examine the flow of everything. When the dynamics of a group are healthy, the members will trust one another, they will treat one another in an equitable manner, and they will hold each other accountable for their actions.

The practise of pointing fingers and shifting blame is an indication that there are issues with the dynamics of the group. People taking credit away from each other and then pointing the finger of blame at each other as soon as anything doesn't go according to plan is a classic example of dysfunctional group dynamics. This is evidence that they do not sense the cohesion of the alliance; in other words, they do not feel like they are a part of a team. A strong group is able to make decisions collectively that are not only effective but also expeditious and do not cause any of the members' feelings to be damaged.

When I was in Europe doing volunteer work around fifteen years ago, I was at a meeting to decide what game we were going to play the next day. The memory of that meeting will stay with me forever. We decided to have a conference that lasted for eight hours in order to choose a game that would only last for ninety seconds. Even though the majority of the members of the group got along well with one another, this was an indication of an extremely inefficient team that had accomplished very little as a whole. Everyone worked towards their own individual objectives, and everyone promoted the game that they considered to be the most successful. Even when I pleaded, "Let's just choose one, come on, we are wasting time!" they insisted on continuing to argue. This proposal was shot down because other people believed that achieving various goals was more important than meeting a deadline for a project. It is impossible to have a productive meeting about what your aim is when there are five, six, or eight people in attendance, all of whom are working towards various objectives, let alone actually achieving anything.

The creative potential of a group is significantly increased when its dynamics are strong. People are feeling more at ease when expressing their thoughts and coming up with new ones. We have all been in the high school or college classroom where the teacher tries to start a brainstorming session, but no one wants to go first; no one raises their hand because the first person to raise their hand is perceived as the teacher's pet, so there are negative social consequences for joining the activity being led by the teacher. The exact opposite is what we want to see in our working environment; we want our staff to feel at ease bringing us awful ideas. It does not matter how terrible the thought is; it will still build up to moments of genius, and we will never get to those moments of brilliance if individuals are never allowed to voice those terrible ideas in the first place.

Influence And The Ability To Motivate Others

The ability to influence others is crucial to and absolutely necessary for effective leadership. It is not due to deceit or other forms of manipulation. Regardless of the official authority position you have, you can still persuade people to act in a certain way on your behalf if you have the ability to guide them in that direction. Your ability to lead must be able to convince a wide variety of people in order to be successful. You are required to argue in a logical manner and come up with reasonable solutions. Before you can successfully persuade your audience, you need to have a solid understanding of who they are. Who exactly is watching your show? When we speak to people of different social classes or professional backgrounds, we deliver a distinct message. Take into account the profession. If you are trying to convince a clinical practitioner of something, you will centre the conservation effort on a method that is relevant to medicine. When speaking with a mechanic or an engineer, you should relate the topic to the specific duties that come with their occupation. Understand your target demographic and communicate effectively with them.

What are the benefits to me?

The message that an audience should focus on the most is the value that may be gained from participating in the effort that you are presenting. The benefit must be something that can be seen, touched, or otherwise physically experienced by the customer. What benefits are there for the group? Why should they take their lead? Consider the efforts from every conceivable perspective. The following are potential advantages of this approach:

Reduced number of procedural steps

Elimination of work that has been done twice

Developing an automated method in order to do away with manual labour

hence making time available for pursuits that are more enjoyable.

enhancing the existing safety records

Rank and public acknowledgement

These are only a few possible advantages, but there are many more. There are an infinite number of advantages. In order to choose the most effective approach, we need to get to know the members of our team. The first step in getting to know our team is figuring out what drives each member of the group.

The motivation that one feels is directly proportional to their level of drive. The requirement to continually increase both the bar and the status quo is one of the best indicators of motivation. The fact that you are reading this book demonstrates how motivated you are to strengthen your leadership skills. People that have high work standards, are goal-oriented, and are committed to continual professional development are seen as individuals like you. Motivation is contagious. People tend to gravitate towards other individuals who share their values and perspectives. You are among illustrious company. In order to motivate your team to perform at a higher level, you need to understand your team and capitalise on the engagement of the individual members. The level of engagement within a team can be measured by the degree to which its members are dedicated to the accomplishment of the organization's goals or values, to contributing to the overall success of the business, and to putting forth their utmost effort on a daily basis. The amount of engagement that each individual member of the team brings to the table will be unique and will likely change depending on the activity that is currently being carried out.

A corporation loses approximately 28 percent of its disengaged team members each year, whereas just 4 percent of employees are highly engaged in their work. In many cases, the decision to leave is not motivated by financial concerns. Consider the effects of being forced to find a replacement for an individual, such as an increase in workload, extra time spent in downtime and training for new employees, the possibility of fragmented care or improper patient management, and patients who quit following treatment programmes.

The opportunity before you is to capitalise on your leadership abilities in order to propel engagement among the members of your team. To begin, we determine the three levels of participation that are present among the members of the team by meeting them where they are.

Individuals who are highly engaged not only think about their jobs during working hours but also think about them outside of those hours and do not regard their jobs to be "work." In general, these individuals make your job simpler. They are receptive to new ideas and ways of doing things. They never stop working towards their objective and are continuously on the lookout for new prospects for advancement.

Consider those who are reliable workers and who give high-quality output on a consistent basis as engaged. Individuals that are invested in their work are crucial to the success of any team. These are the bees that do the actual work. These people are content with the work that they do and have little interest in taking on extra responsibilities. They do not actively participate in the process of developing the model but rather behave as followers of the direction you establish.

Individuals who are not aligned with the position, team, mission, etc. are examples of those who are disengaged. people who require a lot of upkeep, who aren't very productive, etc. They have the potential to bring the team down. They frequently demand a significant amount of your attention and management time. These individuals have the potential to divert the team's attention away from the final goal, to generate turmoil, and to raise the drama inside the team. Your team will likely become anxious as a result of this.

Which category best describes the majority of your team? In most cases, ten percent of employees will be extremely engaged, eighty percent will be engaged, and ten percent will be disengaged. In order to make the most of engagement, you need to be aware of your present standing with your team. Request their candid comments without expecting anything in return. It is essential to your development as a leader over them. You will be aware of the areas in which you require improvement in order to concentrate on your own personal growth. Instill in your team the value of providing you, as their leader, with feedback on their performance. The crew should be rewarded for their feedback. Always keep the partnership and the process of evolving together in mind.

Altering the team's culture rather than developing new programmes is what needs to be done in order to get everyone on board. The only effect that programmes have is to ensure that your most talented employees continue to grow while the rest of the workforce maintains business as usual. When there is anything in it for them, an individual who is motivated to work hard will do so, whereas an individual who is involved in their work will work hard for the sake of the firm. Every leader has the goal of cultivating a working atmosphere that is so appealing to potential new team members that they can't help but be recruited. The concept of respect encompasses a wide range of values, including acknowledgment, empowerment, positive feedback, partnership, expectations, consideration, and trust.

For The Purpose Of Deciding

When unpleasant things happen to you, treat yourself with kindness. Give yourself praise whenever something positive occurs. You can use this strategy to assist you in making judgments, no matter how big or how small. Imagine you are offering guidance to a close friend or family member. In a time of crisis, what advice would you provide to a loved one who is close to you? Repeat these phrases to yourself. Practice self-love.

Always keep in mind that you are great just the way that you are. When we choose to disregard our own hopes and ambitions, we are implicitly telling ourselves that we do not deserve happiness. When we ignore what it is that we truly desire and instead strive to fit ourselves into the mold of someone else's vision of perfection, we unintentionally cause misery for ourselves. You are unique among all people. There is no point in wishing you were someone else; instead, you should focus on becoming the finest version of yourself that you can be. Being honest with yourself is a powerful thing, and it has the additional benefit of assisting you in significantly improving the quality of the relationship you have with yourself.

Never beat yourself up for having negative feelings. Because they don't want to offend other people or cause other people's feelings to be hurt, a lot of people stuff their feelings down or act as if they don't have any feelings at all. But why is it that the feelings of other people are given greater weight than your own? Why would you want to repress your feelings of rage or anguish simply so that someone else can avoid experiencing the same emotions? This does not mean that we should intentionally make other people angry or sad so that we can feel better about ourselves; rather the opposite, in fact. The most important thing is to be truthful with both ourselves and our feelings. Also, keep in mind that everyone is responsible for their own internal experiences, including their sentiments and emotions. If you tell someone that you are upset and they respond by becoming angry too, then the problem lies with the person you told. You are not to blame for the manner in which other people respond to your feelings. Never make the mistake of thinking that you can permanently repress your emotions. We are all capable of experiencing rage, pain, and depression. It's normal to have those feelings. Accept and embrace them as an integral part of who you are. Feel them to the depths of your being, and

61

wallow in them if that's what you want to do. As long as you do not give in to unfavorable feelings about your emotions and allow them to become exaggerated in your head, the feelings will pass quickly and no longer be a problem for you.

You have to make a point of telling yourself how amazing you are and how grateful you are to have yourself in your life. Learning how to express thankfulness to oneself is a skill that is essential but may at first appear to be ridiculously simple. Put your attention on the wonderful qualities that you, personally, have to give. When we pay attention to something, our attention and our energy are automatically directed toward that object. Therefore, if we concentrate more on the positive aspects of who we are, we will use more effort working to improve ourselves. However, keep in mind that the majority of your time should be spent working on the internal you rather than the external you. Your outward look is nothing more than the husk that your spirit inhabits while it travels around the world. Your intellect and your spirit deserve more respect than your physical self, so show them some love.

Never lose sight of the fact that you are a human being. On this planet, there is not a single non-human being. None of us will ever reach the level of perfection. It is important that we do our best, but realistically, that is all we can hope for. We are not perfect; in fact, we frequently get things wrong. In addition, we should never be more critical of ourselves than we are of other people. If you are willing to accept a shortcoming in your neighbor, you should also be willing to forgive same shortcoming in yourself. We all have our own particular insecurities, and at some point or another, each of us has experienced a sense of vulnerability. It is inherent to the human condition. Learn from it, accept it, and appreciate its presence in your life.

There are rocks in this flow that obstruct the link between the two sides. These are referred to be instances of empathy. The letters "B.L.O.C.K.S." These things teach the child that they shouldn't feel the way that they do and that they shouldn't put their faith in their hearts. They are presented here.

F - Frustration

The feeling of boredom needs little explanation. You show no interest in the child's feelings when they share them with you. You don't bother looking at them; instead, you continue washing the dishes, watching television, reading, playing games on your phone, messaging, or doing whatever else you were doing.

After a long day at work, I would pick up my son from school, and while we were driving home, I would check my phone every few minutes. My workday came to a conclusion at the same time as his because we were both located at the same school. After a long day of being in an environment with children and sitting in meetings one after the other, I was finally able to check at the texts on my phone. Therefore, when he came home from school, the first thing he would see was me using my phone. Even though I wasn't on the phone for the remainder of the evening, he kept saying, "Mommy, you're always on your phone!" despite the fact that I wasn't.

When he repeated that statement one too many times, I understood why he had that opinion. When he got into the car with me after a hard day at school, he required my complete and undivided attention. Instead, I gave him a grade of B for boredom. This made it clear that he was not intriguing and did not warrant my attention in any way.

L - Lectures given

When we lecture a child in response to their feelings, this creates another barrier between us. If they bring up the fact that they received a poor grade on their schoolwork, we immediately respond by saying, "This is because you didn't study hard enough."

Or, if we discover that they haven't eaten their lunch and they complain that they're still hungry, we can tell them, "You're supposed to eat three big meals a day! Do you have any idea how much I put in your bag? If you don't eat at the appropriate times, you'll find that your power wanes, and you won't be able to participate in the game. Do you have any idea how many malnourished children there are in Africa who would give their last breath for the meal that I've prepared for you? Why haven't you been eating?!

It's possible that a child is exhausted and yawns. "How many times have I advised you to get an early start on your bedtime routine? Going to bed and getting up at a reasonable hour is a habit that will bring you health, riches, and wisdom. If you go to bed early, not only will you be able to give your body the rest it needs, but you will also have the energy to get through the rest of the day.

We continually lecture our children; the more feelings our children have, the more we need to lecture them to rid themselves of those feelings. In the end, don't you think it's vital for us to share the knowledge and experience that we've gained? Other than that, how else will they learn? When we lecture to our children, we are making the assumption that they are not clever and that their emotions are meaningless, sentimental, and inconsequential things that need to be extinguished out of them. The act of lecturing is a significant barrier to empathy and should be avoided wherever possible.

The Undesirable Repercussions That Result From Getting Angry

Keep in mind what I said earlier: we all make decisions in life, but the ramifications of those decisions are rarely, if ever, in our control. We are going to have to make amends for our angry outbursts and actions sooner or later. Earlier, I discussed what transpired after I was approached by the fire chief as a result of my rage. After a while, the monthly meetings with my battalion chief were discontinued since both he and the chief were pleased with the advancements I had made.

The testing for the job of battalion head was carried out by our department in July of the following year, in 2003. A written exam, an oral presentation, a tabletop tactical exercise in front of a group of fire chiefs, and two separate interview panels were all a part of the procedure. I was chosen as one of the top three candidates for the post, but I did not receive the promotion. Why? They assured me that I was qualified for the post and that they were confident in my ability to fulfill the responsibilities of the job. The fire chief, the division chief, and my battalion chief. On the other hand, not nearly enough time had gone for me to demonstrate to them that I had genuinely prevailed in my battle with anger. Even though it was a difficult and unpleasant pill to swallow, I understood where they were coming from. The good news is that when I re-evaluated for the position of battalion head in 2005, I was successful and was subsequently promoted to the role.

The effects of rage on one's health are yet another negative fallout of the emotion. Problems with one's health can manifest themselves in a variety of ways, including the cardiovascular, neurological, digestive, or immune systems, amongst others. There is also a higher possibility of developing hypertension, a heart attack, a stroke, and ulcers in the stomach.23 In the end, we have to ask ourselves if it is truly beneficial to become enraged and erupt like a volcano. The following is what it says in James 1:19-20: "So then, my beloved brethren, let every man be swift to hear, slow to speak, and slow to wrath; for the wrath of man does not produce the righteousness of God."

People are less likely to interact with us when we are angry, and they are much less likely to approach a leader who is angry because of the latter's unpredictable conduct. One such instance took place while I was serving as a lieutenant at our primary fire station. This was before I was promoted to the position of battalion chief. I frequently fielded phone calls from firemen working at different stations who wanted to know how the battalion chief was feeling at any given moment. When I answered the phone, I was, in essence, serving the same purpose as one of two flags that can be seen at the shore during hurricane season: one of them indicates a tropical storm warning, while the other one indicates a hurricane warning.

If you are constantly criticizing, berating, and yelling at the individuals who work for you, you can rest assured that they will shut down and be very hesitant to communicate with you. The tension you feel toward your subordinates is developing a wedge between you and them. In due time, not only will people begin to mistrust you, but they will also make every effort to stay away from you.

Anger has a detrimental effect on all aspects of our health, including the physical, the spiritual, the emotional, and the mental. Every day, fury carries on its destructive mission, bringing an end to marriages, friendships, professional connections, prospects for growth, and a great many other areas of life that can be joyful. Do not transform into that individual. If this describes you, please know that there is still time for you to change your behavior. If you allow anger to control your life, you will never be able to be a good partner, father, friend, or leader. There is simply no way. It would be wise for us to pay attention to what Thomas Jefferson had to say when he stated, "Nothing gives one person so much advantage over another as to remain always cool and unruffled under all circumstances."24

Consulting Skills That Are Essential To Have

Now that we've discussed the characteristics that make some of the best consultants, let's take a look at the consulting talents that are most in demand and how they apply to the field of human resources:

Thinking creatively: Being creative is a key priority in a variety of different areas. The term "creative thinking" covers a far wider range of activities than you might at first suppose, despite the fact that many different fields may not appear to be likely to prioritize such activities. People that think creatively are able to generate ideas that are superior to the conventionally acknowledged approaches to conducting business in any sector. It fosters the practice of idea generation as well as the listening to the perspectives of a diverse range of people. In the context of leadership recruitment, we see this competency as being particularly beneficial when thinking about how to target certain talent pools or how to extend the pool, particularly when searching for talent that is underrepresented.

Thinking both conceptually and practically: If you think conceptually, it shows that you are a forward-thinking innovator and a visionary. You might have a strong sense of intuition or the capacity to extract ideas from others who have trouble finding the words for abstract notions. Either way, these are valuable skills to have. In order to encourage others to think conceptually and come up with motivating touchstones for the organization for which you are now working, you may facilitate a group brainstorming session by asking thought-provoking questions.

After you have defined your vision, using your talents in practical thinking will enable you to assist others in translating that vision into items that can be acted upon and deliverables that can be produced. It's possible that you may assist in outlining a particular strategy that helps narrow a company's emphasis. You will be able to assist them in organizing projects into component components and assigning duties on the basis of general principles that have been adapted specifically for the organization.

This ability is useful in a variety of different settings within the realm of recruiting. It might be how you help the client recognize what they are actually looking for in the role, or how you help them crystallize their thoughts into an actual role description. Either way, it is how you support the client. In a similar vein, it might be utilized in the process of transforming the requirement of the company into a talent research plan.

Solving problems is a significant part of your job as a recruiter, and there are times when you may not have a lot of background information to draw from in order to find solutions to the challenges you face. It's possible that among the most valuable abilities you can possess are those that allow you to attentively listen to the worries of other people, react promptly to those issues, and intelligently provide potential answers. Even though it should be evident that you need this skill — given that your job is to help your customer solve business challenges by locating brilliant new leaders — it is important to highlight that the topic also comes up in interactions with prospects and applicants. How frequently do you need to make a course correction during a conversation with a candidate in order to alter your framework in response to an unanticipated problem or newly revealed motivation?

Communication that is both comprehensible and empathic: When you have found a solution to an issue, everyone will appreciate your ability to convey your thoughts in a way that is clear, succinct, and shows empathy. We often have the experience of creating candidate treatises that were (in our minds) great, intelligent, and well-reasoned, with several critical questions articulated at the end, only to learn that the client was only reading the first three lines! We can't stress how crucial it is to communicate "clearly and concisely" enough; either keep it to a few bullet points and ask pertinent questions, or give the most relevant information first.

Collaboration with employees at all stages of the job: When dealing with the stakeholders and employees who will carry out the recruiting plan, you will need to have a sense of confidence whether you are acting in the capacity of an internal or external consultant. Any situation in which you find yourself will benefit from your ability to cultivate poise, courtesy, friendliness, outstanding listening abilities, and public speaking skills. You should treat equally important people, such as the building receptionist and the CEO of a publicly traded firm, with the same level of respect during the course of a single day. You never know who you'll be speaking with next. In a similar vein, in many companies you will be working in partnership with members of your own team as well as members of extended teams (for example, HR business partners, executive compensation, and relocation teams, if you're an internal employee), in addition to a wide range of executive leaders. As the owner of your own space, one of the most important skills you may have is the ability to collaborate effectively with everyone.

gaining a new perspective on things

One of the business leaders that I was teaching was wringing his hands and expressing feelings of being stifled and frustrated by the limits that the pandemic had placed on his former method of conducting business. He wasn't a "big fan" of video conferencing and instead preferred in-person interactions with his most important clients and staff, where he could give them a bear hug, shake their hands, look them in the eye, and shake their shoulders. Even more so, he believed that continuing his custom of bringing those folks out to bars and restaurants after their business meetings was an essential part of ensuring that he would continue to have positive relationships with others.

The realization that our lives are fleeting, combined with an awareness of the potential that lies inside each of us, will instill in us a sense of urgency that compels us to make the most of each and every moment. His Holiness the Dalai Lama

During our coaching sessions, we focused on his willingness to answer the question "What's good about this new reality?" with a positive response. He came to the conclusion that not having to travel allowed him to have more time for meaningful talks and to interact with people on a more frequent and in-depth basis. These were the people whose relationships were most important to the success of his company. He discovered that he could connect with a great number of people he hadn't been able to see before the pandemic by using Zoom, Skype, and the phone (once he became accustomed to using these technologies).

"What Happens If I Lose My Job?"

One of the high-tech managers I coached often worried that he would be fired from his position. There was a significant amount of restructuring taking on in both his industry and company. The possibility that he would be affected by it turned into a dread that polluted his days and prevented him from getting quality rest at night.

I asked you, "Tell me about your fear," and you responded. "What is it that you are afraid of?"

"There's a chance I'll be fired," he remarked.

I was curious and asked, "What would happen to you if you lost your job?"

"I'd be completely devastated," he remarked.

I turned and scrawled the word "DEVASTATED" in large characters on the whiteboard that was hanging on the wall.

I prompted him to consider the meaning of the word in the context of his pessimistic imagined future, in addition to his current disposition and frame of mind. I brought to his attention the fact that "devastate" can imply either "to ruin" or "to lay to waste entirely." It would be razed to the ground and cease to exist, just like a house that has been destroyed by a tornado or an earthquake.

If he were to lose his job, do you think he'd be devastated? No, he came to understand. He would look for work elsewhere. What kind of person would he be if he weren't devastated? "Uncomfortable," he admitted after some thought. "If you were willing to put up with being uncomfortable for a while, is it possible that you could find a job that pays even better?" "Is there a chance that you could find a job that pays even better?" "Yes," was his response. "There is a good chance that it will happen."

By exchanging apprehension about the unknowable for curiosity, we free ourselves to explore an endless number of possibilities. Either we may become childlike in our curiosity, stretching our limits, leaping out of our comfort zones, and accepting what life throws in front of us, or we can let fear rule our lives and allow it dictate our every move.

So, his fear-producing thought—"I'll be devastated if I lose my job"—was, after being in a safe coaching zone where he could look inward for the truth, no longer producing fear in him. Instead, he discovered that his "knowing" what would happen wasn't even true.

This process of being curious and practicing self-inquiry is one way of separating leaders from their worrying egoic mind and helping them relax and expand into their innate wisdom. This approach was made famous and accessible by the spiritual teachings of

Byron Katie and is used by many coaches today, including me. With practice, this work can alter who the leader is *being* in their unique circumstances: the owner of their life.

Instead of a fragile, vulnerable, little ego, a leader chooses to be seen as more fully human, experiencing their real being as a larger, wiser, and more creative energy field—a whole person, leaning into and even thriving on change.

People who hold a fixed mindset, on the other hand, have a tendency to assume that intelligence does not change through time. As a consequence of this, they will frequently:

Make an effort to appear intelligent. They are afraid of being judged and appearing to be ignorant. As a consequence of this, they put in a significant amount of effort to give the impression that they are smarter or more knowledgeable than they actually are. This, in turn, inhibits them from learning the information that they need to learn in order to advance to the next level.

Steer clear of problems. They avoid putting themselves in tough situations because they are under the impression that they do not have sufficient capabilities and are terrified of making a mistake.

It's so easy to give up. They have no faith that they can get better, therefore they eventually quit up much sooner rather than later.

Consider your efforts to be fruitless. They perform an assignment below the level of their ability. One reason for this is that, should they give it their all and still be unsuccessful, it would be conclusive evidence that they do not possess sufficient intelligence. This terrifies them more than anything else, and because they believe their capacities are fixed, it indicates that there is nothing they can do to change the situation. They would much rather ignore the problem altogether than face it head-on and risk failing.

Ignore feedback that could be used to improve. Any form of criticism is interpreted as a challenge to their self-esteem by them. It merely "proves" what they already "know," which is that they are not nearly as good as they have the potential to be. Again, because they don't think they can become better, any feedback they receive is meaningless to them. It will simply make them feel worse about themselves.

The success of others should make you feel insecure. These are the types of people who are continually measuring themselves against others to gauge their success. They have the misconception that there is a finite amount of success and that when others get it, it is at the expense of their own. People who have a fixed mindset are more likely to feel inadequate when they are surrounded by others who appear to be more successful than they are. This validates the worst of their concerns, which is that they aren't good enough. As a consequence of this, they would much rather surround themselves with people who have not achieved as much success.

Where do you stand? Which of the two mindsets—a fixed mindset or a developing mindset—do you have?

Always keep in mind that you are a perpetual student, and the first thing you need to do in order to reach your full potential is to adopt a growth mindset. Learning is always an option. You are never finished learning. There is always room for growth.

Culture In Companies: The Process Of Creating And Destroying History

Culture is a phenomena, a state, a predominating set of work protocols, the base of communication network basis, leadership (and following), and consistency: culture is holistically followed by each and every member of the company with unique approach apropos the leadership ladder. Different personnel strata, such as the chief executive officer, manager, engineer, or skilled worker, are all able to witness and participate in the company's culture. When we have a culture that is well-defined, we have a corporate family, and members of that family work together toward a unified goal—in this case, the development of profits. The culture is weakened and contaminated whenever an employee or group of employees attempts to infiltrate the culture on a divisive political basis (low-level or high level), involving the concept of caste, creed, region, religion, ethnic origin, dress code, language, or sex. This causes the culture to become diluted and polluted. The end effect is that good individuals leave the corporation, bad people receive facilitation (and they populate the corporation), and the profit margin for the corporation decreases. It is the responsibility of the business leadership to instill the defined corporate culture among the company's workforce in such a way that no employee will ever consider acting in a way that would disrupt the culture. A suitable corporate mechanism ought to be defined for this purpose. In order to sustain the mission of the corporation, there should always be checks done on violations of the corporate culture.

The perspective of psychology: Cognitive talents and disabilities, when combined with organizational behavior and accountability, subscribe to the essence of the corporation, which is then reflected in the eyes of its employees. Depending on whether the leadership has a biased or unbiased attitude and the level of work ethics that are prevalent, the environment at work will either improve (in which case it will excite the employees in general) or it will deteriorate (in which case it will destroy the employees' capacity to do their jobs and their interest in doing so in general). Every type of communication that's involved in the process of carrying out a work forecasts integrity among employees, and that integrity becomes imprinted on the'subconscious mind' of the employees. The subconscious 'data-collect' in the mind of the employee gets projected consciously penetrating through the employee group or subgroup, and the same is reflected in the culture of the business entity as a whole. Employees who are irrational and biased infect their other employees, which disrupts the culture of the company and creates obstacles for the company's growth. On the other hand, employees who have a rational and unbiased attitude (with healthy cognition) cultivate a nice ambiance within the employee circles, and as a result, construct the corporate culture in a favorable way, which allows the corporation to rise quietly. Conflicts among employees and unfriendly working environments can be a drag on business expansion. In order to ensure that the company culture is maintained over time, an analytical and psychological calculus should be mapped onto the workforce.

Corporate Lesson: The corporate management team (Human resource) should figure out the undefined set of work protocols, the undefined employee feedback mechanism, the undefined differentiation module, the undefined professional communication, and the undefined departmental executions so that the work culture presents itself optimally and no employee (employees) feel harassed (in abusive, disguised work ambience). This idea ought to serve as the "holy grail" of the company's culture to be adhered to.

Are You Working On Your Posture? Examine Your Reflection Carefully In The Mirror

Okay, so maybe a mirror isn't the best option, but you should definitely shoot a full-length photo of yourself from both the front and the side. When you have your photographs, compare them with the following checklist to identify and correct any posture issues that may have arisen.

Are you able to place your ear in front of the area where your shoulders meet in the middle? If you answered yes, then your head is in an abnormally forward position.

If you can see the blade of your shoulder, this indicates that your back is arched too far forward.

When your hips thrust forward, this causes a substantial arch to form in your lower spine. An anterior pelvic tilt is the term that's used to describe this ailment.

Take a gander at your shoulders. Is there a discernible difference in height between the two? It certainly shouldn't.

Do the backs of your kneecaps face inward?

Are there more than ten degrees of inward or outward pointing on any of your toes?

If you have rounded shoulders, you should execute the following exercises:

Lie on the floor with your face down and your arms bent at a right angle with your hands towards the floor. Raise both of your arms by drawing your shoulders back, and hold the position for five seconds without changing the angle of your elbows. Every day, you should complete three sets of fifteen repetitions.

Unable to move the head freely due to a tight neck:

To stretch the back of your neck, move merely your head and bring your chin closer to your chest. This will allow you to move more freely. Maintain this position for five seconds, and then repeat the exercise at least ten times every day.

Shoulder alignment issues or shoulder elevation:

Place your palms down on the seat of the chair you're sitting in while keeping your arms completely straight out in front of you. Now, without moving your arms, press down on the chair until your hips lift up off the seat and your body rises. You should be able to do this without having to move your arms. Keep this position for the next five seconds. Every day, you should complete three sets of fifteen repetitions.

Being There

The ability to change the course of events by one's presence is frequently the quality linked with charisma that is sought after the most. It is common practice to gauge someone's social standing and level of influence based on the quality and force of their presence. Being present in the moment significantly improves the quality as well as the depth of your presence; but, what exactly does it mean to be present? The orientation of our brains and the way we think naturally alter from moment to moment, and these adjustments in thinking can be brought on by almost anything. In order for us to maintain our presence in the here and now, we need to be conscious of our mental states and rid ourselves of any negative habits that we may have picked up along the way. We all, during the course of our lives, acquire behaviors, such as selfishness, boasting, temper tantrums, tardiness, and an overall lack of dependability, that have a detrimental impact on how others view our existence in the world. We have an obligation to remain vigilant in the search for these unfavorable characteristics and to eliminate them as soon as we identify them. The most accurate indicator of our mental condition is our emotional state; the question is, how can we accurately assess our own emotions? And how exactly does this alter the presence that we have? The degree to which we are present in the here and now is directly proportional to the quality of our thoughts, which in turn determines how we are feeling at any given instant. Our thoughts, in order for us to "be" in the present moment, have to be directed toward the here and now, rather than either the past or the future. Here's how your feelings and the passage of time connect with your current state and being in the here and now:

The act of reflecting on one's history might trigger the emotion of anger in a person.

Sadness, like anger, is a sign that we are dwelling on the past (in fact, anger is sometimes referred to as the "bodyguard" of melancholy).

When we ponder about what might happen in the future, we experience feelings of fear and concern.

If you are happy and at peace, as well as having the impression that time is 'flying' by, this is a resounding sign that you are fully present in the moment.

In a nutshell, if we want to be fully present in the now and now, we need to direct our thoughts toward the here and now rather than the past or the future. When we are totally present, we are able to concentrate on and enhance the overall impact of our presence. This impact can be strengthened by the following: making meaningful eye contact with every person there when entering a room, accompanied by a pleasant smile. When we are fully present, we are able to focus on and enhance the overall impact of our presence.

Let the other people speak first, and don't be in such a hurry to start talking yourself. Everyone will have time to acclimate to your presence if you just remain silent for a bit. If your audience is fidgety, give them some time to settle down before you start speaking.

To bring yourself into the here and now, start by closing your eyes, then taking a full breath and holding it for five seconds. When you feel the wind on your skin, direct your attention to different parts of your body: first your left arm, then your left leg, then your right leg, and finally your right arm. Your attention will refocus on the here and now as a result of this.

Those who have presence exude energy, but the question is: where does this energy originate? Both our actual and our perceived amounts of energy can be increased by tapping into one of two major energetic forces that exist within each of us. Do not let your anxiety and self-doubt cause you to waste the energy that comes from your psychical self, which is the state of preparedness and alertness that your complete body is in. This is where our energy comes from. Second, we get our energy from our own unique identities, which includes both our life experiences and our individual personalities. Our acts receive a multiplicative boost of energy from our own selves when they are aligned with the principles and emotions that guide us in life. If we find that we lack the drive to complete a task or scenario, we need to realign our values with either the situation or the work at hand. When our values cannot be matched with our proposed task or course of action, or when they are in direct opposition to it, the suggested task should either be reformulated or rejected.

5. Inspire and uplift the heart. The hearts and minds of constituents need to be encouraged. Leaders are responsible for ensuring that followers understand the advantages of engaging in behavior that is congruent with deeply held beliefs.

1. To set an example for others involves engaging in behaviors and engaging in practices that are founded on guiding concepts and ideals. By actively upholding a set of core principles, a leader can boost their own personal credibility. Behavior that is consistent and displays a leader's commitment to the values and guiding principles that are advocated is essential to successfully modeling the way for others. Character is the primary consideration in modeling. The lives of leaders are guided by their guiding ideas and beliefs, and they make a personal commitment to working toward achieving those ideals.

To set an example for others to follow implies having the confidence to behave in accordance with what God reveals rather than merely reacting to the arbitrary demands of the people. A leader, once persuaded that a particular course of action is the one that should be taken, must have the determination to continue down that road of action and remain unafraid even as the situation becomes more demanding and tough. Kouzes and Posner are adamant that leaders' beliefs and principles should serve as the foundation for the development of their vision (Leadership Challenge 15). Because the leaders' guiding principles and values are reflected in the vision, the leaders themselves have faith in the vision. Christians look to God as their primary source of direction in life. It is expected of Christian leaders to develop and believe in visions that reflect and convey the goals and values that God has for his creation.

Following the vision that God has given them to pursue is a model for other Christian leaders to follow.

2) Communicating that a leader knows where he is headed, conveys it in a way that is clear and concise, and cares about it passionately can be accomplished through inspiring a shared vision. Individually, God calls people to leadership, which enables those leaders to perceive God's vision and enables those leaders to become personally involved in God's dream for his people. Collectively, however, leaders pursue God's goal for his people, turning the individual calling into a group pursuit through vision sharing. Leaders have the responsibility to present the vision to the people and to explain it to them. Leaders inspire individuals to spend their lives in achieving important changes by sharing their vision with others and encouraging others to do the same. Others are influenced by the vision, and it also encourages change.

In the context of the church, having a vision involves not just drawing in new members but also imitating the example set by Jesus. A depiction of what God has planned for the future is called a vision. (As God's will dictates) Joining God in what he is already doing and what he wants to do in his church is what the process of developing a vision entails. Sharing the vision has as its ultimate purpose the invigoration and stimulation of the body of Christ to adhere to the teachings of Jesus. It is essential for the leaders of the church to dream God's dream and cast God's vision for the church. The leaders of the church agree with and obey God's plan. "The gift of leadership is the divine capability to cast vision, motivate, and direct people to harmoniously accomplish the purposes of God" (Bugbee, Cousins, and Hybels

90).This definition of leadership comes from the book "The Five Dysfunctions of a Team" (Bugbee, Cousins, and Hybels). Alterations are going to take place as the trip continues for both the leader and the constituency. The manner in which objectives are achieved and tasks are finished can be complicated by change.

3. Challenging the process requires leaders to engage in innovation, take risks, and continue to learn from their experiences. Innovating, growing, and making improvements are all results of challenging the process, which in turn challenges the way things are done and may result in the company being reinvented. Pioneers, early supporters of innovation, adopters of new ideas, and change agents are all characteristics of leaders. According to Slaughter 101, God works via human instruments to bring about transformation. Each of the great biblical figures Abraham, Moses, Jesus,

and Paul served as a change agent for God throughout their time on earth. Leaders who can act as change agents are the most effective agents of renewal.

The Confident Head Of The Pack

A person who is optimistic is one who has the conviction that everything will work out for the best. It is vital for one to have a positive attitude regarding a specific undertaking in order for one's performance to be enhanced by perseverance. It should also be underlined how important it is to keep a positive work atmosphere in order to boost the morale of everyone on the team and encourage high-quality performance.

Positive thinking is essential for leaders to possess in order to provide them the ability to find answers to difficult questions and devise ingenious strategies. A pessimistic thinker would give up on a project and scrap it because they have lost hope that the project will be successful, whereas an optimist is someone who never gives up easily and knows that one who never gives up easily. You are aware of the common proverb that asserts, "the plan can always be changed, but the goal should never be changed."

A leader who is optimistic is someone who feels that the team will be successful in whatever it does and works toward achieving that success themselves. Because he or she is aware that people are more dedicated to achievement when they are happy doing what they do, this leader projects a pleasant mood that mixes pleasure with productivity. When this happens, the activity that needs to be completed transforms into something that the team truly wants to carry out.

The Process of Becoming One:

Because so many leaders are susceptible to falling into the trap of becoming cynical, there are a significant number of books and movies centered on awful bosses. Because you most certainly do not want someone to write a nasty book about your poor leadership skills, you need to continuously remind yourself of the following advice on how to be an optimistic leader:

Concentrate on finding solutions. When anything goes wrong, one of the worst things that human beings do is look for someone to blame, even when there isn't actually anyone to blame. This is one of the worst things that humans do. You should steer your team to concentrate on how to fix the problem instead of pointing fingers at each other as an optimistic leader if you want them to follow your lead and be productive.

Be receptive to constructive criticism; in order to be an optimist, you need to be able to accept bad feedback gracefully and avoid becoming defensive in response to it. Maintaining your composure in the presence of someone who is providing feedback to you is a skill that can be practiced, and you should use the feedback as an opportunity to grow and learn. At first, achieving this level of success may be challenging for you, but over time, you will get better at it.

Emphasize the positive developments. The optimistic leader is someone who is always able to discover some positive aspect, no matter how negative the situation may be. Always begin and end the conversation on a positive note, and consider any impediments to be merely challenges that your team is capable of overcoming. Instead of feeling discouraged and helpless after the conclusion of the meeting, everyone will have exited the room feeling empowered and thrilled.

One of the most important ways of thinking that optimists have is that they see unpleasant situations as singular instances rather than as examples of a larger pattern. If an optimist were to make a mistake while giving a presentation, for instance, they would believe that the only thing that is required of them is to learn from their error and do better the next time. On the other hand, a pessimist would start to believe that they are not excellent at giving presentations, and this would have an effect on the activities that they take in the future. Be careful not to wallow in regret over past errors.

You Absolutely Need To Have Passion.

First and first, you have to be passionate about what it is that you are doing or what it is that you are attempting to do. A significant number of leaders lack passion. They are preoccupied with the benefits, such as money or bonuses, that can be obtained from the employment. They are woefully ignorant of how vital it is to invest their hearts and minds in their work and communicate that enthusiasm to the members of their team.

Think about it this way: if you do not feel passionate about what you are doing, what is the point of continuing to do it? And how could you possibly expect other people to be enthusiastic if they can plainly tell that you are not enthused about the subject matter yourself?

If it isn't already clear, one of the keys to success is to follow your passions. If you are just starting out in the business sector, for example, you should search for a profession that will not only allow you to maintain your current standard of living but will also encourage your mental and spiritual development. If you enjoy what you're doing, it won't feel like work even when things get challenging. Love what you do. It will be much simpler for you to rise to the position of outstanding leader from here on out.

With a fervent...

You will assist other people in understanding that it is acceptable to pursue what it is in life that they desire. Some individuals are of the opinion that they should forget about what it is that they truly desire and instead make do with what is now accessible. That is not correct. If you want to be a great leader, you need to show other individuals that it's okay for them to go for their goals. A great leader is someone who motivates others to stay true to who they are in spite of the challenges they face. If someone is honest with themselves, they will have more chances to improve themselves, and as a result, they will be able to motivate and encourage those around them.

You won't have the feeling that you're "working," but you'll still perform to the best of your ability no matter what you're doing. When you are engaged in an activity that you are enthusiastic about, it rarely seems like labor. It's a lot of fun to try your 'best shot' at something. Pressure is transformed into enthusiasm, expectations into objectives, and accomplishment into a sense of accomplishment and satisfaction.

You will have a sense of satisfaction and joy. Imagine that you have a passion for cooking and decide to build a restaurant of your own, or at the very least, begin working right away toward launching a restaurant someday. You won't consider this endeavor to be work at all because you have such a passion for the kitchen and because you are always seeking for new methods to improve your culinary techniques or come up with delicious new dishes. In this way, not only do you get to work with what you love, but you also have the opportunity to share your talents with the world, which will ultimately lead to a sense of accomplishment and satisfaction on your part.

You will become an expert in the activity that you are engaged in. Naturally, if you enjoy what you are doing, it will be much simpler for you to perform to the best of your abilities. You start to wonder about it. Your expertise and knowledge base will grow, which, in turn, will fuel your excitement and motivation.

Great results open doors to previously unimaginable opportunities. Your outcomes will mirror the level of enthusiasm you put into whatever it is that you are working on when such feelings are present. Never settling for less than their best, great leaders always start with excitement and passion for the work they are doing. They provide the best outcomes as opposed to results that are simply "okay"; once you are able to accomplish this consistently, more people will admire and appreciate you, and more people will be willing to follow you as a result.

Keep in mind that it is really crucial to be enthusiastic about the work that you do, not only in this day and age but especially in this day and age. Remember it, and you won't veer from the path that leads to success!

Next, it is important to discover how you may talk to your subordinates in the appropriate way, which will allow you to have the most productive conversation possible. You can find out more about this topic in the following chapter.

Being attentive

The ability of listening is considered the second most important social skill that is required for excellent leadership. It's a common misconception that listening and hearing are interchangeable, however this is not the case. Hearing is the process of registering noises that are occurring all around us but are only picked up on the surface by our brain.

Because of this, a significant portion of hearing is comprised of sounds, such as the horns of passing vehicles, the chirping of birds, people arguing, background music, and so on.

Hearing and listening carefully.

However, listening is an even more profound activity than hearing. It is referring to the sounds that we decide to focus more of our attention on, to the point where we command our brain to let those sounds permeate to its more profound depths. To illustrate this point, let's say that we make the decision that, for whatever reason, we would like to examine the chirping of a specific bird in greater detail. Therefore, rather than allowing the chirping to passively exist on the surface of our brain and fade away, we command it to migrate deeper into the layers of our brain that are currently active. In this section, we take a more in-depth look at the sound, analyzing aspects such as the frequency at which the chirping occurs, the octaves at which the bird is chirping, and other noises that the chirping is similar to.

Awareness of detail.

As a form of communication, listening requires the listener to pay undivided attention to what is being conveyed by the speaker. A leader must first listen to the words, and then take in their significance in order for his brain to understand it. He is required to consider the speaker's comments and come up with responses that are suitable. It is not uncommon for a speaker's words to appear to convey one meaning on the surface, but when looked at from a more in-depth perspective, they can be seen to convey an entirely different meaning. at instance, if a manager schedules a meeting at eight in the morning and a female employee tells him in a perturbed tone that it's too early for her, she is not actually making a comment; rather, she is simply not making a comment. She is trying to make the manager aware of the difficulties she has in coming to office at that early hour, and requesting a later time for the meeting or permission for her to come into the meeting later. Good social skills on the part of the manager require him to pay attention to what she is saying on a deeper level. The Hindu scriptures talk about three different levels of spiritual practice. The first one is called shravana, which translates to "listening." The second stage is called manana, and it means paying attention to the text and thinking about what it means.

To educate.

Listening is an important social skill for leaders because it allows them to learn about the challenges, concerns, and desires of their followers. This is a significant benefit of listening. If the manager follows the example of the female worker and pays close attention to both the words she says and the way she carries herself while doing so, he will acquire knowledge about the ways in which employees report for work and the challenges they experience in doing so. Because of this, he has the potential to develop into a more understanding and, thus, a more humanitarian individual. To make things a little less difficult for his employees, he has a lot of different choices accessible to him. In the end, he will be regarded as the model of a good leader, and this will contribute to the charisma that he possesses as a leader.

People That Are Submissive Are Devoted.

Those who submit to authority are loyal to the authority in question. To be loyal means to stand with your leaders through good times and bad, regardless of the circumstances. It indicates that you will defend the reputation of your organization's leaders and speak positively about your own company.

There are circumstances in which loyalty does not equate to agreement. You can have a respectful disagreement with someone who is in a position of authority over you while still maintaining your allegiance to them. The world sees any kind of disagreement between a leader and their followers as a sign of treachery and betrayal, no matter how small. On the other hand, no two people will ever reach the same conclusion. Because we are unique individuals who possess distinct mental processes, we will perceive and comprehend the world around us differently. In addition, you should not even expect to agree with every choice that is made by your leaders since you should not even expect to agree with them.

When you disagree with the leader, you can politely communicate your perspective with them, but you must also be willing to obey him if he does not change his mind. This is what it means to be loyal. In my opinion, showing more dedication to one's cause is demonstrated through openly and respectfully disagreeing with any authority figure than through keeping one's disdain of that authority a secret. Some people will go to a meeting, but they will maintain their silence while the decisions are being made. Then, after the fact, they mutter and complain about the choices that were made. They will not be able to adhere to the plan in its entirety. This is not simply a breach of loyalty but also an act of defiance. Either show loyalty to the organization or resign from your position.

6. Those who are submissive show respect.

You are commanded to "respect those who work hard among you, who are over you in the Lord" (1 Thessalonians 5:12), as it is written in the Bible. This verse is directed specifically toward leaders of churches, but it can be applied to anybody in a position of leadership.

Leaders are deserving of respect. The role of leader is one that is challenging and time-consuming. It requires an investment of both time and effort on your part. Numerous meetings, individuals who need to be visited, and a mountain of other incidental activities are required of leaders. It can be a very draining experience for leaders to have to attend to the requirements of all of their followers. You must show them that you appreciate them by praising the effort that they have put out.

Not only do those in positions of leadership need to be respected due to the challenging nature of the work they undertake, but also because the Lord has placed them in positions of power. Simply because they hold that position does not signify that they are superior to you or have a higher level of education. It simply implies that according to the position they occupy, you owe them respect because of their status.

It is extremely difficult to exercise effective leadership if one does not have the respect of one's followers. When you stop showing respect for your leaders, you are actively working for their demise. They deserve the respect you give them. Don't keep it from them! If you make the decision to show respect for your leaders on your own volition, they will be less inclined to demand that you do so.

Furthermore, 1 Thessalonians 5:12 instructs believers to love and respect those in authority over them. You are obligated to show respect for the position, regardless of the specific individual who now occupies it. To reiterate, this does not imply that you are required to agree with everything that is communicated to you by your leaders. And you should not, under any circumstances, ignore the presence of sin in their lives. However, you are obligated to hold them in the highest regard. What exactly does this mean, and how can you go about carrying it out?

a. You can demonstrate respect by keeping your mouth in check.

You may show respect for those in charge by keeping your mouth in check, which is one of the greatest methods to do so. Make a pact with yourself that you will never talk poorly of any of the people in authority in your community, including those in your church, your household, your workplace, and your country. You ought to be willing to make this commitment with regard to any individual. Do not get together with other people to discuss or evaluate different leaders.

In front of your children, you should avoid speaking adversely about the leaders of the church you attend. After attending church on Sunday, some parents may go straight home and have "roasted Pastor" for lunch, during which they will publicly criticize their pastor in front of their children. A person who comes into a church with a bulldozer and tears down the walls does less damage than someone who speaks ill of the people who serve as the leaders of the church. The same thing takes place in a lot of staff rooms and at water coolers at corporations.

Take Advantage of Their Predilection for Computers and Socializing With Others

You have to go on to the next part of the process once you have successfully built a good relationship with your Millennial employees, provided them with opportunities for growth, and begun to leverage their talents. The next step is to capitalize on their amazing affinity for modern technology and networking.

This is the method that can be used to complete this stage.

Include the Technology that they are utilizing in their Workplace in yours.

Organize a meeting with your millennial employees and ask them about the many technical devices, software, applications, and developments they use in their personal or professional lives. Additionally, ask them how you can integrate these technologies into the working environment. This encounter is going to turn out to be fairly significant for you professionally, and it is going to assist you in revolutionizing your organization.

For example, if you have no experience with Pinterest or any of the other social media forums that can assist you in advertising and promoting your company, you can consult with Millennials about how to boost marketing strategies by making the most of these platforms. You will be able to make use of their enthusiasm for technology in this way, which will give them the impression that they play a significant part in the operation of the business and encourage them to put in even more effort.

Leverage their enthusiasm for making connections.

Engage in conversation with the millennials who work for you and bring them along to a variety of social and professional activities. Because of this action, you will enhance your reputation as a leader and forge a closer connection with the millennials who make up your workforce, both of which will be to the great advantage of your organization.

The people are the most important aspect of leadership.

Everyone is affected by this, unless your business is entirely automated and only deals with other automated businesses. People are the most important aspect of your business model, regardless of whether your company is run by people or whether it sells to people. This is true regardless of which scenario applies to your company. Therefore, they are entitled to be shown the highest possible regard.

If your workers believe that they are valued and appreciated, they will put in 10 times the effort that they would put in if they believed that they were undervalued and used. "People Quit Bad Bosses, Not Bad Jobs" is the subtitle of this book, and it couldn't be more accurate.

In my time in the military, I witnessed a number of instances in which good soldiers deserted their posts because of abusive superiors. This has a domino effect and will snowball.

People will leave an organization because of a poor manager, and the more people who leave, the more work the remaining workers will have to complete; as a result of the increased workload, some of these workers will decide to leave the company as well. When this happens, the corporation is forced to pay out of its own funds to educate additional employees. Avoid having this occur in your company by demonstrating gratitude to those who have helped you.

Action: Have someone organize a day for the team to bond, such as a trip out to go karting or paintballing, and then follow it up with a meal together afterward. If you wish to, you can take care of the organization yourself. If you can find someone to organize it for you, that person can include it in their annual report to demonstrate that they are capable of getting things done.

The eighth lesson is that it is okay to admit when you've made a mistake.

Everyone has a fallible human nature, and it is only natural for humans to occasionally make mistakes. One of the most important qualities of a good leader is the ability to admit when they are wrong and take responsibility for their actions. Don't point the finger at anyone else or make an effort to cover it up. People have tried to cover up their mistakes in front of me before, but it always ends up becoming a bigger issue. It takes a strong person to be able to put their hands on their heads and admit, "I was wrong." It takes an even stronger person and a lot of courage to be able to do this in front of all of your employees.

If you demonstrate by raising your own hands, it will be much simpler for your employees to follow suit. It is much simpler to correct an error when it is caught early on, before it has had the chance to snowball into a significantly more serious issue. It is easier to deal with these types of situations if you just come out and say what you need to say rather than sitting down for a significant amount of time. Therefore, you should just come out in front of all of your employees and hold your hands up by doing this. Keep in mind that you are leading by example and putting some of the other points of good leadership skills into play by doing this.

Take Action: There is not a whole lot more to say about this other than the fact that you should admit your mistakes sooner rather than later.

The ninth lesson is that together we are strong.

The power of 10 minds is greater than the power of one mind. Employees have provided some of the most innovative ideas for some of the largest companies in the world, and it helps businesses function more effectively when their workforce is cohesive.

I have mentioned in the past how our manager took the time to sit down with all of us and discuss both the positive and negative aspects of working there. This is a principle that should be followed by all businesses, regardless of their size. It is your responsibility as a leader to bring the members of the workforce together.

Take action: Make it a goal to hold at least one meeting a week or once a month at which members of the staff can discuss issues or share ideas. If you do this, you will strengthen the unity of the workforce, leave people with the impression that they are valued and appreciated, and make improvements to your business.

To me, this is such a no-brainer that the only possible outcomes of these meetings are positive ones; therefore, you should go into work tomorrow and organize the first meeting of the employees.

The outing for team building can also be an effective way to bring the staff closer together.

The tenth and final point is that there is always room for improvement.

The expansion of both the company's operations and its revenue should be the primary focus of any business, regardless of its current size. There is no such thing as a perfect company, and there never will be; regardless of how large your operation is, there is always room for improvement. Employees are also included in this category of people.

Training and mentoring your staff will be beneficial to the company, so make sure to provide them with these opportunities. All of these things— keeping employees in the company, being an effective leader, showing your employees that you support, appreciate, and value them, and making people feel valued— contribute to a robust company ethos.

This also applies to 'yourself.' A wise man once said that you should invest at least 10 percent of your annual salary in your education.

Keep in mind that a leader is someone who helps employees improve while also encouraging them.

Implementing a training program for your employees can help improve the quality of their work as well as provide them with a general education.

Make arrangements to attend a class so that you can improve your own education.

Increase the amount of time you spend reading, particularly non-fiction.

Educate Yourself On The Traditions Of The Working Environment

Another thing that a great leader should keep in mind is how essential it is to have a deep comprehension of the culture that their organisation possesses. You need to have an understanding of the kinds of products that the people around you want, as well as the reasons why a particular product or service succeeds in a particular culture but fails to succeed in others.

People's means of making decisions, the way they speak and communicate with one another, the tales they tell their children and grandchildren, the myths and legends that are passed down, and the methods of doing work are all fundamental components of culture. It is also about the customs and mannerisms of a certain location or nation; however, in this case, we are speaking about the culture of your workplace.

It is also believed that culture is something that can be learnt and that it reveals a great deal about the manner in which the people who live in a particular location behave. What really crucial is that you gain an understanding of the culture of the location in question so that you can determine what it is that you have to give and so that you can learn more about the people who are in your immediate environment.

This chapter will teach you all about how to understand your culture and create the greatest kind of goods and services for your people. There are specific methods in which you could understand your culture, and you'll discover all about those ways.

Taking a Look At

The first thing you need to do, just like anything else in life, is to watch your culture, because doing so will allow you to accept and comprehend it, and it is the only way to do this. In order to accomplish this, you need to:

Take a look at the activities going on in the area around you. Check out what others have displayed on their workstations or walls, observe what they are wearing, and make an effort to learn what it is that they enjoy to listen to or watch in their spare time. In this manner, it will be simple for you to comprehend what has a possibility of working and what does not, and it will be simple for you to devise goods and services that will be beneficial to the individuals concerned.

Observe the behaviour of your followers in their interactions with one another. You will gain an understanding of what drives them or what causes them to become agitated in this manner. As you can see, the people around you are pretty much a symbol of the individuals you would like to follow you or patronise your products, and as a result, it is absolutely crucial that you know what they want and what they do not want.

Look for hints that aren't being said. You read in a previous chapter about the significance of non-verbal communication; you should work on improving this skill. You should educate yourself not only in the art of nonverbal communication for yourself, but also in the art of interpreting the nonverbal communication of those who are in your immediate environment.

Taking Stock

The next thing you need to do is take inventory of the area around you. You are able to accomplish this by asking specific sorts of questions, such as those that will help you better understand things and will be able to guide you towards making a decision about what it is that you could do. The following are some examples of possible questions:

Where exactly are all of the many departments that make up your office located?

What kinds of things do people keep on their workstations?

What are some common topics of conversation during breaks?

What do people talk about in their e-mails and letters to one another?

How frequently do individuals use their phones, other electronic devices, and computers?

How would you characterise the tenor of your messages? How do you communicate with other people? Do you present a nice demeanour or do you intimidate them?

What kinds of films and television shows do they enjoy watching? Which songs are now enjoying a lot of success?

What sorts of garments do they put on their bodies?

What can you notice hanging on the walls or posted on the bulletin boards?

What kinds of foods do individuals enjoy eating?

What kinds of things do individuals do in the various regions of your office?

What kind of reactions do people have towards you and towards one another?

What exactly are the contents of your memos?

Discussions Through Interviews

You are aware of how crucial it is to conduct interviews with potential employees before hiring them and incorporating them into your business, right? Well, interviews are also crucial if different individuals are already working in your firm, so that you would know how people are getting along with each other or if there is something that needs to be changed. This would allow you to know how people are getting along with each other and whether or not something needs to be changed. inquiries such as, "Who do people consider to be a "hero" or someone worth emulating around the office?" are examples of sample inquiries.

146

If there was one thing in the office that needed to be altered, what would it be and why would it need to be changed?

Which values do you feel are most important for your employees to uphold? How would they like to see these values reflected in the work that they do and how would they like to see it done?

Do they believe that these ideals still hold significance in today's world?

What do you think is the most impressive aspect of the organisation?

What do you think is the most impressive quality that the employees possess?

Why do some errors occur, and how can we stop them from happening in the future?

What is the single most telling sign that the business won't succeed?

Re-organization of Cultural Practises

You'll be able to determine whether or not any sort of change is required after carrying out interviews and performing an analysis of the current state of affairs. Reorganisation of cultures is possible through the following means:

Having an understanding of the culture that you now have and basing your future endeavours on what you have picked up from the people in your immediate environment are two important steps. As this is a significant choice, you should keep in mind that you should not decide on your own and instead solicit the feedback of those who report to you.

Make a decision regarding the direction you wish to take your firm, as well as the qualities or services you would like it to represent. Consider the ways in which this new vision can benefit the firm as well as the ways in which it might be compatible with the culture that you are now a part of. Testing your ideas in the market is absolutely necessary in order to determine whether or not they have a chance of being successful in the long run.

Ask yourself what you might be able to do with this new vision, and then inquire of the people who follow you about their reactions to it. If none of you have any reservations about it, then you should go with the mission; but, if you get the impression that the majority of your followers are uneasy about it, then you should call off the expedition because it is unlikely to be successful.

And make the necessary adjustments to your behaviour so that others will be inspired to do the same. You, as a leader, should be the one to initiate the change. You should have faith that this shift will result in positive outcomes and that it is feasible for you to achieve your goals if you all put in the necessary effort.

Observe, evaluate, and conduct interviews before attempting to reorganise your culture. This will ensure that you get the most accurate picture possible. Don't be in a hurry to make a choice.

The Science and Art of Persuading Others

"I couldn't care less what other people think of me," she said.- Theodora "Teddy" Roosevelt

It is a good thing to allow these words to serve as a source of inspiration for you, as well as to help you gain perspective over yourself and realise that you do not care what other people think of you. However, there are some people whose opinions you should care about in some way, such as your boss, coworkers, and of course, your family and close friends, in order to retain equal respect in all of your interactions. This includes your family and close friends, as well as your family and coworkers. Even though most people don't actively seek to exert their influence on others, the fact of the matter is that everyone does it, regardless of whether or not they are aware of it.

Because it's not simple to do, purposely swaying the opinions of other people is an art form. It requires effort since you have to learn how to observe and interpret the behaviour of other people. Think about initiating contact with an existing or prospective client of a corporation. If you are unable to read them, you will be unable to figure out how to interact with them in a way that is beneficial to either you or your organisation. If you are unable to communicate effectively with others, you will be unable to successfully negotiate with them or add weight to whatever it is that you are attempting to sell or convey. Those who are skilled in marketing and sales are experts at persuading others to take their point of view. They are well aware of both the appropriate and inappropriate things to say in order to capture the attention of others, maintain that attention, and accomplish the goals they have set for themselves.

You have the ability to convince people, just like an excellent sales or marketing expert would. You can acquire the skills necessary to approach people and become familiar with the things you should say in order to get the most out of a meeting. The ability to influence others can be used not only to enhance the quality of your work experience and the results you achieve, but also to facilitate the development of new connections and strengthen current ones. When you are able to successfully influence other people, you open the door to a variety of possibilities, some of which may be positive while others may be negative. You have a talent for gravitating more towards the good, and you can use it to make the lives of the people around you better. You will earn greater respect for doing this, and if you are someone who is already in a position of leadership, you will be seen as a more authoritative person because of this.

You can successfully influence individuals by following a number of steps, including the following:
First, you need to provide individuals with what it is that they want.

If you want to successfully influence people, you should focus on providing them with what they want rather than what you desire. Respect and trust can be built into a relationship by showing the other person that you care about what they desire. It builds trust between you and the other person by demonstrating that you care about what it is that they want. Because people like to do what they want to do, rather than necessarily what you want to do, being selfless makes you more likeable because people like to do what they want to do. You do not need to always do what other people want to do, but if you want to have a favourable influence on other people, you will find that doing so in a moderate amount will improve your relationship with those people. It may be quite challenging for you to do this task if you are a self-centered person; but, if you are not one of these people, satisfying the needs and desires of others will come naturally to you.

The following are some short and easy pointers that can assist you in accomplishing your goal: - Admit both your mistakes and your frustrations.

Remember to take notes and educate yourself by observing the errors of others.

If you want to communicate more effectively, keep what you say as straightforward as possible. This can be accomplished by not trying to be too careful and instead being more direct with what it is that you want to communicate rather than being overly careful and trying to dance around your message.

- Incorporate positive elements, such as feelings of motivation or experiences that are uplifting, in order to provide new and exciting chances for value addition and expansion.

You will become like the people you spend the most time with, so surround yourself with successful people. Those who you spend the most time with will become your reality.

-       Turn your attention away from yourself and towards other people in order to earn respect, but avoid trying to persuade others. Try to be subtle about it, and find out more about what you can do to help other people.

Step 2: Place a strong emphasis on the significance of the individuals with whom you are interacting.

People are essential, particularly those individuals with whom one interacts frequently and professionally. When you are in a position of management or leadership, which puts you in control of other people, you will become aware of how your employees or team reacts to you. When you go out of your way to make other people feel important, they will respond by going above and beyond what is required of them. In addition to this, they will perform the task without any difficulty. When people have the sense that they are valued in their occupations, they don't view their work as a burden or as something they have to do to keep their positions. When people feel appreciated, they are more likely to not only fulfil the bare minimum of what is expected of them but also to go above and above in their work. When you treat people as though they are important, even in your personal life, they will treat you with a lot more respect, regard you to be a trustworthy figure, and give more to you in return. This applies even if you treat people as though they are important in your professional life.

www.ingramcontent.com/pod-product-compliance
Lightning Source LLC
Chambersburg PA
CBHW071646210326
41597CB00017B/2134